POWERFUL
MUSCLE CARS

by Cheryl Blackford

Consultants:
Sammy and Marsha Allen
American Muscle Car Club
Panama City, Florida

CAPSTONE PRESS
a capstone imprint

Edge Books are published by Capstone Press,
1710 Roe Crest Drive, North Mankato, Minnesota 56003
www.capstonepub.com

Library of Congress Cataloging-in-Publication Data
Blackford, Cheryl.
Powerful muscle cars / by Cheryl Blackford.
pages cm.—(Edge books. Dream cars)
Includes bibliographical references and index.
Summary: "Discusses American muscle cars, including their history, how they are
restored and customized, the most popular models, and how muscle car owners
enjoy their cars with shows and races today"—Provided by publisher.
Audience: Age 8-14.
Audience: Grades 4 to 6.
ISBN 978-1-4914-2012-6 (library binding)
ISBN 978-1-4914-2183-3 (eBook pdf)
1. Muscle cars—Juvenile literature. I. Title.
TL147.B57 2015
629.222—dc23   2014021517

Editorial Credits
Carrie Braulick Sheely, editor; Heidi Thompson, designer; Pamela J. Mitsakos, media
researcher; Katy LaVigne, production specialist

Photo Credits
Alamy: © ClassicStock, 15, © epa european pressphoto agency b.v.28–29, © Motoring
Picture Library, 11, © picturesbyrob, 9, © Performance Image, 21, © Mark Scheuern,
24–25; Corbis: © Bettmann, 7, © Car Culture, 5, Transtock/ © Robert Genat, 16–17, 23,
© Tony Savino, 27; Dreamstime: © L Hill, 7 inset, © Dana Kenneth Johnson, cover, ©
Raytags, 12–13, 19, 20; Getty Images: Science Source/Zwiazek Margaret, 18

Design Element: Shutterstock: David Huntley Creative, iconizer, Seamartini Graphics
(throughout)

Printed in the United States of America in Stevens Point, Wisconsin
102014   008479WZS15

Table of Contents

AMERICAN MUSCLE

The loud rumble of the engine. Tough steel expertly crafted into sleek lines. Glistening paint. If you see a muscle car, you might notice any of these features. American car companies built muscle cars in the 1960s and early 1970s. Muscle cars were more than just a way to get around. They had power, speed, and style. These powerful cars attracted many young drivers. Today the cars—now much rarer—still attract thousands of car enthusiasts, both young and old.

Stock car racing fueled the muscle car craze in the 1950s. People flocked to watch *NASCAR* races on tracks such as Florida's Daytona International Speedway. Ford, General Motors, and Chrysler all wanted their cars to win NASCAR races. The company leaders felt that people would be more likely to buy the models that won on the racetracks. The companies built powerful engines to increase the speed of their cars. They also experimented with the cars' designs. The manufacturers' plans worked. People raced to buy the cars they saw speeding around the tracks.

Music and movies drew more attention to muscle cars. Ronny and The Daytonas sang about Pontiac's blazing GTO in their hit song "G.T.O." Wilson Pickett's song "Mustang Sally" recognized Ford's popular Mustang. The Beach Boys sang the lyrics, "She's real fine, my 409" about the Chevrolet Impala SS 409. In a famous car chase scene from the 1968 movie *Bullitt*, the hero drove a green Mustang. He chased the villain's black Dodge Charger. This car chase has nearly nine minutes of roaring, tire-squealing excitement.

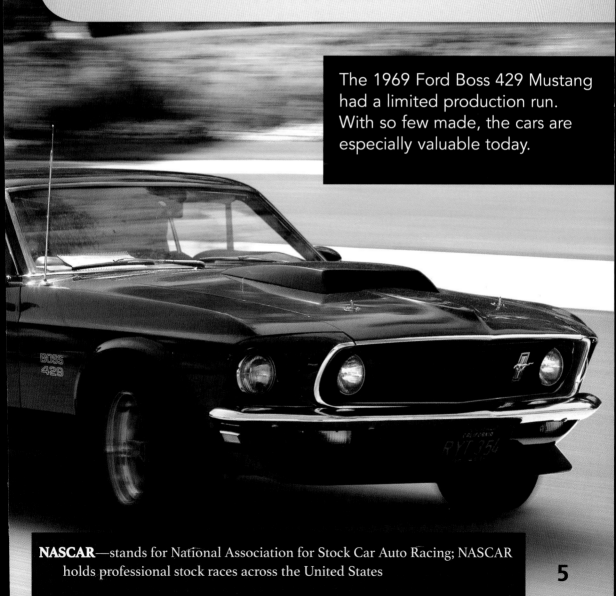

The 1969 Ford Boss 429 Mustang had a limited production run. With so few made, the cars are especially valuable today.

NASCAR—stands for National Association for Stock Car Auto Racing; NASCAR holds professional stock races across the United States

A HISTORY OF SPEED

Which car was the first true muscle car? People still argue about that. The Oldsmobile Rocket 88 came out in 1949. It quickly set records on the NASCAR circuit. Chrysler introduced the C-300 in 1955. The convertible's claim to fame was a powerful V-8 engine called a Hemi. But experts think the first true muscle car was the GTO. Pontiac introduced this speedster in 1964. Nicknamed "The Goat," this car was a thundering beast. It had a massive V-8 engine and blistering speed.

In the early days of NASCAR, race cars had original factory parts. For this reason, they were called stock cars. Ordinary people could buy these cars and drive them on the streets. Car companies battled to design stylish stock cars with powerful engines that would win races.

Under the Hood

What led muscle cars to victory? In many cases it came down to power. Most muscle car engines had eight *cylinders* arranged in a V shape. These engines are called V-8s. Muscle car engines were internal combustion engines, like most of today's car engines. A mix of air and gasoline is squeezed into the engine cylinders. Sparks from the spark plugs set off small explosions, igniting the air and gasoline mixture. The *transmission* uses the power created by the engine to move the wheels.

A car spins out during the NASCAR International Sweepstakes race in Daytona, Florida, in 1959.

1965 Pontiac GTO

cylinder—a hollow area inside an engine in which fuel burns to create power

transmission—the series of gears that send power from the engine to the wheels

Big Engines, Big Power

Chrysler introduced its V-8 Hemi engine in 1951. Called the FirePower, its cylinder heads were shaped like half a sphere—a "hemisphere." That's why the engine was called a Hemi. Cars with Hemi engines won so many races that the Hemi was banned from **NASCAR** in 1965. The huge Chrysler 426-cubic-inch Hemi produced a thrilling 425 *horsepower*. It powered the top three cars in **NASCAR**'s 1964 Daytona 500 race.

Engines are called big-block or small-block depending on their size. Ford offered tame six-cylinder engines for its early Mustangs. Buyers who wanted more power could choose a small-block 289-cubic-inch V-8. But by 1968 Ford offered a big-block 428-cubic-inch engine for its Mustang. Called the Cobra Jet, it blew away the competition at the 1968 National Hot Rod Association (NHRA) Winternationals.

Chevrolet engineers designed powerful engines too. Chevy's big-block 409 V-8 engine became an instant **NASCAR** hit. In 1961 the first 409 produced up to 360 horsepower. By 1963 it blasted out 425 horsepower.

Fact

Engine displacement is the amount of air and gasoline mixture that can be sucked into an engine cylinder. When muscle cars were popular, engine displacement was measured in cubic inches. Today it is more commonly measured in liters.

horsepower—a unit for measuring an engine's power

Cars with a 426-cubic-inch Chrysler Hemi engine proved to be tough competitors on the racetracks.

9

Pony Car Rivals

The Ford Mustang was so popular that it gave rise to the nickname "pony car." The nickname came from the galloping chrome horse on the Mustang's grille. Pony cars were fast, cheap, and fun to drive.

Ford introduced the first Mustang at the 1964 New York World's Fair. The sleek white convertible had red bucket seats. The Mustang was not the fastest car around, but it came with many engine options. Mustangs charged off the showroom floors. Ford sold 1 million of them by 1966.

Plymouth had introduced its Barracuda two weeks before the Mustang. This car was a *fastback* that had an extreme slope. The 273-cubic-inch V-8 engine gave the Barracuda plenty of horsepower, but the Mustang was more popular.

General Motors launched the Chevrolet Camaro in 1967 to cash in on the pony car craze. The standard engine was a 230-cubic-inch V-8 that produced 140 horsepower. But the monster 396-cubic-inch V-8 produced up to 375 horsepower.

fastback—an automobile with a roof having a long curving downward slope to the rear

Top Early Muscle Cars

Car	Year	V-8 Engine Displacement	Horsepower	Top Speed	Acceleration (in seconds, 0–60 mph/97 kph)
Shelby Mustang GT350	1965	289	306	126 mph (203 kph)	6.5
Barracuda	1965	273	235	121 mph (195 kph)	9.1
Camaro Z/28	1967	302	290	140 mph (225 kph)	6.9
Shelby Mustang GT500	1967	428	360	132 mph (212 kph)	6.8

*Horsepower numbers may not be exact. Horsepower varied slightly because of certain modifications.

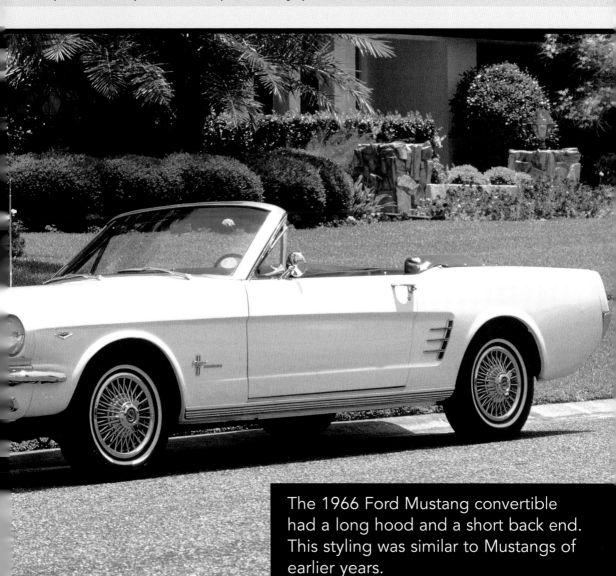

The 1966 Ford Mustang convertible had a long hood and a short back end. This styling was similar to Mustangs of earlier years.

Muscle Car Racing Battles

Pony cars battled one another on the racetracks. The Sports Car Club of America (SCCA) started its Trans-Am Series of *road races* in 1966. In 1969 champion driver Mark Donohue won six of the final seven races in a Camaro. By 1970 all the major carmakers had hired top drivers to race their cars in the Trans-Am Series.

road race—a race that has both left and right turns and is usually held on paved tracks

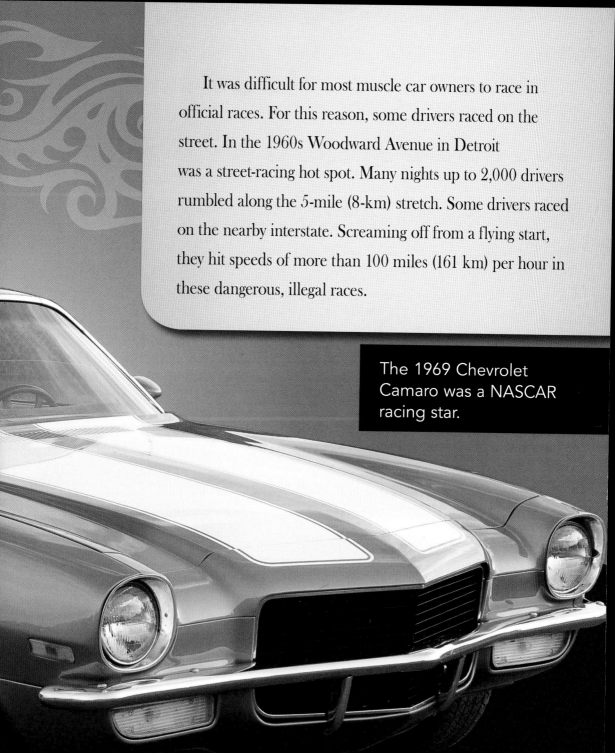

It was difficult for most muscle car owners to race in official races. For this reason, some drivers raced on the street. In the 1960s Woodward Avenue in Detroit was a street-racing hot spot. Many nights up to 2,000 drivers rumbled along the 5-mile (8-km) stretch. Some drivers raced on the nearby interstate. Screaming off from a flying start, they hit speeds of more than 100 miles (161 km) per hour in these dangerous, illegal races.

The 1969 Chevrolet Camaro was a NASCAR racing star.

Illegal street racing caused injuries and deaths. As time passed more racers were drawn to racing on official tracks. Wally Parks had founded the National Hot Rod Association (NHRA) in 1951. The NHRA was a driving force behind the building of many drag strips across the United States. Drag strips are built for drag races. In a drag race two drivers start from a standstill. After receiving a signal to go, they blast down the short drag strip. In a race with traditional rules, the first driver to the finish line wins.

The End of an Era

The year 1970 was the peak of muscle car mania. By 1972 the popularity of muscle cars was fading. Gas shortages sent gas prices soaring. Muscle cars became expensive to run. Their dirty exhaust fumes broke new clean air laws. The devices meant to control pollution from the exhaust decreased the cars' horsepower. Government rules meant new safety features, such as big, heavy bumpers, had to be added to the cars. By 1974 the muscle car craze was almost over.

By the 1970s many drag strips were available for racers around the United States.

ROAD ROCKETS

When muscle cars were common in the 1960s, the big three American car companies were split into divisions. Buick, Chevrolet, Oldsmobile, and Pontiac were divisions of General Motors. Dodge and Plymouth were divisions of Chrysler. Mercury was a division of Ford. Each year the divisions worked to design new muscle cars and attract buyers. In the huge world of muscle cars, certain models rose to the top.

Pontiac GTO

Car and Driver magazine called the GTO "the best American car we have ever driven" in its March 1964 issue. Young drivers flocked to buy it. The stylish 1964 GTO sported *hood scoops*, twin exhausts, and heavy-duty shock absorbers.

hood scoop—the raised part on a car hood with an opening that allows air directly into the engine compartment

Plymouth 'Cuda

The Plymouth 'Cuda was a high-performance version of the Barracuda. The first 'Cuda came out in 1969. In 1970 and 1971 the 'Cuda was king at Plymouth. The car had a massive 440-cubic-inch engine. The engine had the largest displacement of any pony car of its time. The 'Cuda could roar from 0 to 60 miles (97 km) per hour in under six seconds.

The 1971 Plymouth 'Cuda thrilled drivers with its mega horsepower.

Ford Mustang

Mustang buyers could *customize* their cars in many ways. They could choose fancy paint stripes or special grilles and wheel trims. They could have a six-cylinder engine. Or they could size up to a bigger engine. With the 289-cubic-inch V-8 in a 1967 Mustang, they could power from 0 to 60 miles (97 km) in less than nine seconds. With the 390-cubic-inch V-8 engine, drivers could accelerate the car the same distance in seven-and-a-half seconds.

Chevrolet Camaro

Chevrolet put the Camaro on the market in September 1966 to compete directly with Ford's popular Mustang. In 1967 Camaro buyers could choose one of or all three packages offered. These were the Rally Sport appearance package, the Super Sport (SS) performance package, and the Z/28 performance package. With many racing upgrades, the Z/28 package gave buyers a purebred racing machine.

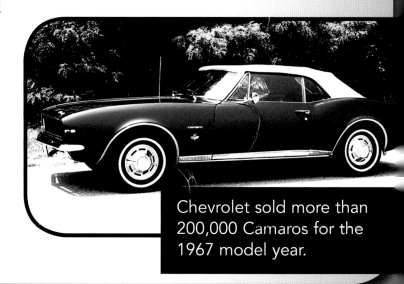

Chevrolet sold more than 200,000 Camaros for the 1967 model year.

customize—to change a vehicle according to the owner's needs and tastes

Dodge Challenger

Dodge launched the Challenger in 1970. It looked stunning with its long hood topped with a hood scoop. Buyers could choose from many style options including bright paint colors with names such as "Lime Light" and "Lemon Twist." Buyers could also choose from different engine options, including the powerful 426-cubic-inch Hemi.

The 1971 Ford Mustang Boss 351 was longer and wider than previous Mustangs.

Dodge Charger

Styled long and low with a short trunk, the Dodge Charger looked like a beast ready to pounce. In idle the car rumbled and rocked. Racing fans drooled over the Dodge Charger R/T with a Magnum 440 V-8 engine. The R/T's top speed was a screaming 156 miles (251 km) per hour.

Dodge Charger

Fact

Plymouth named its popular Road Runner after the famous cartoon bird in the Warner Brothers' *Looney Tunes* TV series. The car's horn made a "beep-beep" sound just like the cartoon character did.

Power to Weight Ratios

A heavier car needs more power to go fast. The power to weight ratio is the power divided by the weight. Faster cars usually have higher power to weight ratios.

Car	Year	Engine Displacement	Horsepower	Weight (lbs)	Power to Weight Ratio
Corvette 427 Coupe	1969	427	435	3,450	0.126
Dodge Challenger	1969	426	425	3,890	0.109
Plymouth Road Runner	1969	426	425	3,938	0.108
Camaro Z/28	1970	350	360	3,640	0.099
Dodge Charger	1967	426	425	4,346	0.098
Shelby Mustang GT 350	1966	289	306	3,158	0.097
Mustang Boss 302	1969	302	290	3,387	0.086
Pontiac GTO	1970	455	360	4,209	0.086

Oldsmobile 4-4-2

The Oldsmobile 4-4-2 blasted eardrums. The name came from its four-barrel *carburetor*, four-speed manual transmission, and dual exhaust. It blasted out 345 horsepower and went from 0 to 60 miles (97 km) per hour in 5.5 seconds.

Oldsmobile 4-4-2

carburetor—a part of the engine that mixes oxygen with fuel before it is forced into the engine cylinders

LIVING THE GLORY DAYS

Drivers who were teenagers in the 1960s and 1970s remember the height of muscle car mania. They remember the roar of the exhaust and the smell of burning rubber. They remember the thrill of cruising through town to show off their powerful cars. Those drivers are part of the "baby boom" age group. Many people in this age group are still muscle car fans. But muscle cars have fans of other ages too.

Today's Treasure

Muscle car owners spend time and money to restore their cars. Restored muscle cars are in high demand, and their values are rising. Restoration often includes rebuilding the engine and repairing the bodywork. Some owners customize the cars or modify them for racing. Many owners repaint their cars in the original colors. Others choose new colors.

Greg Peterson stored his 1971 Hemi 'Cuda in a barn in Illinois for 35 years. He paid about $5,000 for his car. Now it could be worth as much as $750,000.

Gail Wise owns the first Mustang ever sold. She bought her light blue convertible two days before Mustangs were officially available. In 2007 she had the car restored. Gail's car cost her about $3,400 in 1964. Now it could be worth up to $250,000.

Laurie Slawson is a proud Mustang owner who became a national director of the Mustang Club of America. Laurie has restored two Mustangs, including a gold 1968 Mustang coupe.

a restored 1971 Plymouth 'Cuda convertible

Showing Off

Muscle car owners enjoy displaying their cars at local and national auto shows. The Woodward Dream Cruise is the biggest one-day classic car show in the world. More than 1 million people attend the Woodward Dream Cruise each year.

Detroit, Michigan, is called the "motor city" because Ford, General Motors, and Chrysler all have factories in or near the city. Every year the Henry Ford Motor Muster is held near Detroit. The Motor Muster is a car show that celebrates the history of American cars. The Motor Muster has a huge parade of *vintage* cars which were made from 1933 to 1976.

Cars cruise down a street during the 2007 Woodward Dream Cruise.

Racing

Racing and speed were important parts of the muscle car craze. Today drivers compete in many types of races. Many muscle car owners compete in drag races. These races are usually held on $\frac{1}{4}$-mile (0.4-km) or $\frac{1}{8}$-mile (0.2-km) drag strips. Muscle car owners might also compete in autocross races. Autocross races are timed events on a set course. They let drivers test how well their cars handle.

Fact

In 2014 the Barrett-Jackson Collector Car auction set Guinness World Records for large tents called marquees. One record was for the largest marquee at 435,656.95 square feet (40,474 square meters). It took a lot of cars to fill that tent!

vintage—relating to an old period of origin or manufacture

MODERN MUSCLE

Muscle cars are so popular that car companies are building new versions of old favorites. As the new models roll out of the factories, fans debate which ones should win top honors.

Mustang Stampede

Ford celebrated the Mustang's 50th anniversary in 2014. Ford released a limited number of special anniversary cars—1,964 to be exact. This number is the same number of Mustangs Ford originally released in 1964. The new Mustangs have some classic styling features, such as the tri-bar rear lights. They also have advanced electronics, including a blind-spot information system to help drivers while changing lanes.

A New Z/28

Chevy rolled out a new Camaro Z/28 in 2014. Its sleek styling takes cues from the first Z/28s made, including a fender flare over the wheels. Its huge V-8 engine produces a whopping 505 horsepower. The car comes with a high price tag of $75,000.

Onlookers admire the 2015 Ford Mustang at the New York International Auto Show.

An Anniversary for Dodge

In 2014 Dodge celebrated its 100th birthday by wheeling out new 2015 models of the Charger and the Challenger. Engine options for both cars include a V-6 and V-8. The Challenger has special styling details such as big five-spoke wheels and anniversary badges.

2015 CHARGER

A Passion for the Ages

All over the United States, people own and collect muscle cars. Some owners have spent time and money restoring their old cars. Others race to buy the new models that car companies create. These new models deliver the passion of muscle cars to a new generation of fans.

The 2015 Dodge Charger's new styling is based on the Chargers of the late 1960s.

supercharger—a belt-driven system that connects to a car's engine and pushes air and fuel into the engine's cylinders; a supercharger increases the engine's power

GLOSSARY

carburetor (KAHR-buh-ray-tuhr)—a part of the engine that mixes oxygen with fuel before it is forced into the engine cylinders

customize (KUHS-tuh-myz)—to change a vehicle according to the owner's needs and tastes

cylinder (SI-luhn-duhr)—a hollow area inside an engine in which fuel burns to create power

fastback (FAST-bak)—an automobile with a roof having a long curving downward slope to the rear

hood scoop (HOOD SKOOP)—a raised part on a car hood that lets air go into the engine

horsepower (HORSS-pou-ur)—a unit for measuring an engine's power

NASCAR—stands for National Association for Stock Car Auto Racing; NASCAR holds professional stock races across the United States

road race (ROHD RAYS)—a race that has both left and right turns and is usually held on paved tracks

supercharger (SOO-pur-char-juhr)—a belt-driven system that connects to a car's engine and pushes air and fuel into the engine's cylinders; a supercharger increases the engine's power

transmission (transs-MISH-uhn)—the series of gears that send power from the engine to the wheels

vintage (vin-TIJ)—relating to an old period of origin or manufacture

READ MORE

Gifford, Clive. *Car Crazy*. New York: DK Publishing, 2012.

Hamilton, John. *Muscle Cars*. Speed Zone. Minneapolis: ABDO Pub., 2013.

Woods, Bob. *Smokin' Muscle Cars*. Fast Wheels! Berkeley Heights, N.J.: Speeding Star, 2013.

INTERNET SITES

FactHound offers a safe, fun way to find Internet sites related to this book. All of the sites on FactHound have been researched by our staff.

Here's all you do:

Visit *www.facthound.com*

Type in this code: 9781491420126

Super-cool stuff! Check out projects, games and lots more at **www.capstonekids.com**

INDEX